COOKING
THE
SOUTHERN AFRICAN
WAY

Lerner Publications Company
A division of Lerner Publishing Group
241 First Avenue North
Minneapolis, MN 55401 U.S.A.

Website address: www.lernerbooks.com

Library of Congress Cataloging-in-Publication Data

Cornell, Kari A.
    Cooking the southern African way / by Kari Cornell and Peter Thomas.
       p.   cm. — (Easy menu ethnic cookbooks)
    Includes index.
    ISBN: 0–8225–1239–4 (lib. bdg. : alk. paper)
    1. Cookery, South African. 2. Africa, Southern—Social life and customs. I. Thomas, Peter, 1947– II. Title. III. Series.
    TX725.S6C67 2005
    641.5968—dc22   2004011869

Manufactured in the United States of America
1 2 3 4 5 6 – JR – 10 09 08 07 06 05

easy menu ethnic cookbooks

COOKING

culturally authentic foods

THE

including low-fat and

SOUTHERN AFRICAN

vegetarian recipes

WAY

Kari A. Cornell in consultation with Peter Thomas

Lerner Publications Company • Minneapolis

Contents

Introduction

Southern Africa is an area of great beauty and stark contrasts. Diversity abounds in this region, which includes the countries of South Africa, Mozambique, Namibia, Botswana, Zimbabwe, Lesotho, and Swaziland. Giraffes, lions, and elephants roam Botswana's savanna grasslands, while the bright lights of Johannesburg, South Africa, twinkle against the night sky. Early morning fog rolls across dry sand dunes near the Namibian coast, and fishers cast nets into turquoise waters that meet the stunning white sand beaches of Mozambique. As tourists in beautiful Cape Town, South Africa, decide between spicy grilled shrimp and a succulent steak at an upscale restaurant, women in small Zimbabwe villages pound dried corn into coarse grain to prepare porridge for the next meal.

Southern Africa is home to many groups of native Africans, each with its own traditions, culture, and foods. Added to the mix are the descendants of Europeans and Asians who settled in southern Africa. All of these groups contributed languages, religions, customs, and recipes to the area, and southern African cuisine reflects the region's multiculturalism. The traditional African cornmeal porridges, meat-based stews, and samp (hominy corn) and beans have been combined with *boerewors* (homemade farmer's sausages), fish and chips, and delicious desserts of European origins, as well as Asian-influenced samosas (savory stuffed pastries) and curry-spiced dishes. This blend of cuisines makes eating in southern Africa a delicious adventure.

Yellow rice with raisins is a colorful and tasty side dish. (Recipe on page 43.)

INDIAN
OCEAN

Ruvuma River

MOZAMBIQUE

Zambezi River

Harare ★

ZIMBABWE

BOTSWANA

Limpopo River

Windhoek ★

NAMIBIA

Gaborone ★   Pretoria ★

Johannesburg ●

Maputo ★
Mbabane ★

SWAZILAND

AFRICA

SOUTH
ATLANTIC
OCEAN

Maseru ★

SOUTH AFRICA

LESOTHO

SOUTHERN
AFRICA —

Cape Town ●

The Land and Its People

Southern Africa stretches across 1,521,000 square miles of mostly
dry, mountainous land lying between the southernmost tip of the
African continent and extending roughly to the Ruvuma River in
northern Mozambique. South Africa, Namibia, and Mozambique
define the southern African coast, which is washed by the Indian
Ocean in the east and the South Atlantic Ocean in the west. South
Africa is the region's largest and most populous country.

In the tropical, forested country of Mozambique, mangrove trees grow in coastal swamps, and sandy beaches meet waters rich with fish, prawns, squid, and crayfish. Coastal plains extend in a narrow strip southward from Mozambique, all the way around South Africa and northward into Namibia. In southeastern South Africa rises a string of mountain ranges called the Great Escarpment, dividing the coastal plain from the plateaus of the interior. Within these ranges nestles Lesotho, a small, mountainous country completely surrounded by South Africa. Lesotho is home to the mountain Champagne Castle, southern Africa's highest point. Swaziland is another small nation—in fact, tucked between Mozambique and South Africa, it is the tiniest country south of the equator.

South Africa's interior is part of a plateau region known as the veld. Sheep, goats, and cattle graze the veld's dry grasslands. In other areas, farmers grow corn, peanuts, oats, wheat, and fruit. Still drier climates include the Namib Desert in western Namibia and the vast Kalahari Desert, which consumes nearly two-thirds of Botswana. In north-western Botswana, the Okavango River Delta provides fertile soil, but uncontrolled flooding makes it nearly impossible to grow crops.

East of Botswana, lions, zebras, elephants, and giraffes roam the savanna (grasslands) of Zimbabwe. The Zambezi River, tumbling three hundred feet over the world-famous Victoria Falls, separates Zimbabwe

A family plays at the beach in Cape Town, South Africa.

from Zambia to the north. In eastern Zimbabwe, mountains and thick forests dominate the landscape and create a natural boundary with Mozambique. Zimbabwe's mild climate and regular rainfall make it ideal for raising crops, and farmers grow tobacco, wheat, soybeans, peanuts, barley, oats, sugar, coffee, and tea in the plateau's fertile soil.

Southern Africa's history is as varied as its landscape. Historians believe that ancient granite ruins in southeastern Zimbabwe were once the center of the great Shona civilization. The Shona, one of many Bantu-speaking African groups, had first settled between the Zambezi and Limpopo rivers around A.D. 500. At the community's height, between A.D. 800 and 1600, it was the richest and most powerful in southern Africa. The Shona mined gold, exchanging the precious metal for the cotton cloth, porcelain, and glass that neighboring African groups had obtained from Asian traders. At the same time, other Bantu-speaking groups, including the Zulu, Swazi, Ndebele, Pondo, Sotho, and Tswana, lived farther south. Although these groups all spoke Bantu-based languages, each had unique customs and traditions. They carved out their own territories and began to raise crops and herd cattle.

A group called the Khoisan also lived in southern Africa. Originally leading a nomadic lifestyle, the Khoisan hunted wild game and gathered fruits and nuts growing in the area. While on the move, they lived in lightweight, beehive-shaped dwellings made of twigs and brush that could be easily taken apart and transported to the next hunting ground. Eventually, the Khoisan established more permanent settlements and raised livestock for food.

In the late 1400s, Portuguese sailors landed at the Cape of Good Hope (a point in southwestern South Africa) and on the coast of Mozambique. Portuguese traders had long traveled around the Cape on their way to Asia. Eventually, they began using the tip of Africa as a place to rest and replenish their supplies during the long journey. Later, English and Dutch sailors also began using the rest stop. Then, in 1652, a company called the Dutch East India Company established

This illustration of a Khoisan hut was made in 1805.

the first permanent European settlement there. Seeking land for crops and cattle, the newcomers seized property from the native Khoisan. The Dutch eventually won the struggle for land, but the Khoisan refused to work for them. Needing farm laborers, the Dutch began bringing slaves to the region from Madagascar, Malaysia, Indonesia, and India. These peoples came to be called the Cape Malay.

Other Europeans soon joined the Dutch colony. French, Dutch, and German farmers became known as Boers, developing their own culture and the unique Dutch-based Afrikaans language. As more settlers arrived, European-held lands spread well beyond the original Cape settlement, pushing the Khoisan and other native groups farther from their lands. After the British seized control of the settlement in the 1790s, the Boers, unhappy with British rule, migrated inland in the Great Trek of the mid-1830s.

The British enacted laws limiting the freedom of native Africans and giving white European settlers most of the colony's political and economic power. Although Afrikaners (European Afrikaans speakers) took control in 1910, after two wars with the British, British rule had laid the groundwork for a system of racial separation called apartheid, which began in 1948. Under apartheid, South Africans of Asian, African, or mixed-race descent were told where they could live and what jobs they could hold. Nonwhite children were barred from school or crowded into small, dark classrooms where they received minimal instruction. This destructive system affected all of southern Africa.

Apartheid finally ended in 1994, after many battles and years of hardship, struggle, and racial strife. With new leaders and new laws, the vast inequalities created among South Africans of different ethnicities began to change. Nevertheless, southern Africa still struggles with political unrest in some of its nations.

Throughout the region, many black southern Africans still lead very different lives from their white neighbors. In small villages, many black Africans live much as they did hundreds of years ago. Traditional round houses with thatched roofs are clustered together to form small communities. Large families share the same home or live in several homes with a common courtyard. Women cook meals outside over a wood fire. Between breakfast and lunch, they may grind corn with large mortars and pestles or work in the garden. Most families grow much of the food they eat and raise cattle for meat. Children help out by cleaning, carrying water, and watching the herds. Many African men have to work in cities, sometimes traveling hundreds of miles and coming home only on weekends. Fewer white southern Africans live in the countryside, and those who do tend to be wealthier. Some Afrikaner farmers

A woman in Mozambique uses a large mortar and pestle to grind rice.

still tend acres of land on South Africa's veld, growing grapes, wheat, and corn, and raising cattle.

While most southern Africans do still live in rural villages, city life in the region is much like that in other parts of the world. In cities, large differences still exist between the lifestyles of whites and non-whites. However, since the end of apartheid in South Africa, more blacks there have moved into the middle class. Adults go to work in high-rise buildings while kids attend school. Many white southern Africans, along with nonwhites in the growing middle class, live in well-kept suburban homes with manicured gardens.

Regional Cooking

A traveler in southern Africa might notice that several similar recipes are prepared with slight variations throughout the region. In homes all over southern Africa, for example, porridge commonly accompanies a vegetable or meat-based stew. In Zimbabwe the porridge is called *sadza* and is made from cornmeal and milk or water. Some cooks transform this basic dish into a popular vegetarian course called *nhopi* by adding pureed pumpkin, peanut butter, and fresh spinach. In the villages of Swaziland, Lesotho, and South Africa, corn, known as mealies, is often ground and served as a porridge, called *mealie pap* in South Africa and *putu pap* in Lesotho. Millet porridge is a favorite in Namibia and in Botswana, where it is called *bogobe*. Many southern Africans sprinkle sugar on porridge and enjoy it for breakfast.

Pumpkin, yams, grilled corn on the cob, roasted cassava root, spinach, and other vegetables may be served with the porridge, along with stews made from goat, chicken, lamb, beef, or vegetables. Although chicken and beef are only enjoyed on special occasions in small village homes, meat often forms the basis of a dinner in wealthy households. Soup, green salad made with fresh local produce, and fresh fruit such as mango, guava, or melon round out the meal.

The descendants of European and Asian settlers throughout southern Africa have created their own distinctive cuisines. The Cape Malay of South Africa combine the meat- and potato-based recipes of the Dutch, curry seasonings from Asia, and local fruits and vegetables in uniquely delicious dishes. Marinated meats called *sosaties* are grilled to perfection and dressed with tangy fruit chutneys called *blatjang*. *Bobotie*, a curried meatloaf with dried currants, apricots, apples, and almonds, is a South African favorite. In Durban, South Africa, which has a large Indian community, cooks mix spices such as turmeric, cinnamon, cloves, and cardamom to make the curry seasonings that flavor many Indian foods. Favorite dishes include vegetable *biryani* (stewed lentils, carrots, potatoes, tomatoes, and seasonings, served with rice), lamb in a coconut-curry sauce, samosas, and chapati, a traditional flat bread.

Southern Africans of European descent enjoy meats and vegetables cooked over the *braaivleis* (barbecue grill). Boerewors, first made by early Cape settlers, remain popular. Southern Africans usually buy these sausages from local butcher shops, but some cooks still make them from scratch. Grilled kebabs, marinated until tender, are another favorite. Afrikaners even cook stews in the great outdoors, placing three-legged cast-iron pots called *potjie* over a red-hot fire and slowly simmering onions, carrots, tomatoes, mushrooms, and other vegetables with meat and spices. While the stew cooks, diners sip favorite beverages and enjoy conversation with friends. Traditional British dishes, such as roast beef with Yorkshire pudding, cottage pie (beef or turkey potpie), and fish and chips, are also popular in restaurants throughout southern Africa and among those of British descent in Zimbabwe, Botswana, and South Africa.

Mozambique, which was once colonized by Portugal, still displays a strong Portuguese influence on its cuisine, making it unique to southern Africa. Local cooks combine this influence with the abundant seafood for which the coastal nation is known, and large prawns, squid, lobster, and crayfish form the basis of many Mozambican recipes. Shrimp piri-piri, large prawns marinated in a

A woman in South Africa uses a potjie (cast-iron pot) to cook over an open fire.

spicy red pepper sauce and then grilled on skewers, is very popular. In dishes such as *matata*, a delicious clam and peanut stew, clams are cooked in Portugal's famous port wine, mixed with a distinctly African peanut sauce, and served with rice.

Holidays and Festivals

Southern Africa's multicultural mix means that religious and secular (nonreligious) holidays and festivals abound. European settlers introduced Christianity to the region, and Christmas lights brighten city streets in the weeks before the holiday as people crowd the stores to shop for presents. Because southern Africa lies south of the equator, seasons are the opposite of those in the Northern Hemisphere. As a result, the Christmas holiday falls in the summertime, and backyard *braais* (barbecues) are very popular. Foods served for Christmas are not necessarily unique to the holiday, but the abundance of favorite dishes on the table makes Christmas Eve dinner special. Family and friends exchange gifts and eat a buffet dinner that might include yellow rice, samp and beans, Yorkshire pudding, grilled corn on the cob, boerewors, sosaties, roast beef, grilled shrimp, lobster, Christmas cake, and Christmas pudding.

In South Africa, Easter means a long weekend, as most stores and businesses are closed on Good Friday and Easter Monday. Compared to Christmas, Easter is a quiet, solemn affair. Many South Africans spend Good Friday and Easter Sunday at church. Traditional foods include hot cross buns and baked ham.

Nagmaal, which means "Holy Communion" in Afrikaans, is a Christian festival that is unique to South Africa. In the days when travel was slow and farm settlements were far apart, Afrikaners stayed home to pray most Sundays. However, four times each year, families traveled to town for religious services. More than times for worship, these three- to four-day events were major celebrations. Families visited with friends and neighbors, children were baptized, and wedding announcements were made. In modern times, families pile into cars to travel to Nagmaal in the nearest town, where they attend church, catch up with family and friends, and shop for arts and crafts.

Indian and Cape Malay Muslims (followers of the Islamic faith) in southern Africa observe Ramadan during the ninth month of the Islamic calendar. The holiday commemorates Muhammad, Islam's founder, receiving his first messages from Allah (God). Muslims throughout the world show their devotion to Allah during this time by praying and fasting (not eating) between sunrise and sunset. Indian Muslims usually celebrate the end of Ramadan with a great feast, complete with steaming plates of favorite foods such as vegetable biryani, samosas, and curried meat stews over rice.

Hindu members of South Africa's Indian community celebrate Diwali, the Hindu New Year, in October or November. During the festival, which lasts for almost a week, families clean their homes, light oil lamps, exchange sweets, and set off fireworks.

Southern Africans of all faiths typically celebrate New Year's Eve on December 31 with big parties or a night out dancing. On New Year's Day, southern Africans spend time in the summer sun. Festivals, barbecues, picnics, and trips to the beach are all popular ways to celebrate. In Cape Town, people of mixed ethnicity parade through the streets in an annual carnival. Participants sing and dance, dressed in matching, brightly colored clothing.

One of South Africa's biggest celebrations is the festival that takes place each July in Grahamstown. Dance, music, art, and literary readings showcase the work of African, European, and Asian artists who call South Africa home. Crowds of more than fifty thousand people flock to the event to purchase pottery, wood carvings, and original paintings and to enjoy performances. Hungry festivalgoers may snack on fish and chips, roasted corn, or other foods sold at sidewalk stands.

Throughout the region, traditional agricultural festivals celebrate the harvest, prepare seeds for planting, or call for rain. In Zimbabwe, for example, planting and rainmaking festivals begin in small farming communities just before the September rains are expected to begin. A medium—an elder who is believed to have contact with ancestral spirits—oversees the ceremonies. After an evening spent sitting around a bonfire, sipping homemade beer, dining on foods such as *dovi* (chicken in peanut sauce) and *nyama ne nyemba* (steak and bean stew), and singing and dancing to traditional songs, villagers meet the next day at the medium's home. The medium collects crop seeds and asks the spirits to protect them from disease before redistributing them among the villagers for planting. Rainmaking ceremonies soon follow, as villagers dress in traditional clothing and gather for a night of singing and dancing around the medium. In times of drought, rainmaking festivals continue for many days in hopes of bringing forth badly needed showers.

Countries within southern Africa also celebrate independence days to honor the times when their nations were liberated from colonial rule. Citizens typically have the day off from work and celebrate with parades, picnics, music, and fireworks.

Before You Begin

Cooking any dish, plain or fancy, is easier and more fun if you are familiar with its ingredients. The southern African dishes in this book make use of some ingredients you may not know. Sometimes special cookware is also used, although the recipes in this book can easily be prepared with ordinary utensils and pans.

The most important thing you need to know before you start is how to be a careful cook. On the following page, you'll find a few rules that will make your cooking experience safe, fun, and easy. Next, take a look at the "dictionary" of cooking utensils, terms, and special ingredients. You may also want to read the tips on preparing healthy, low-fat meals.

Once you've picked out a recipe to try, read through it from beginning to end. Then you are ready to shop for ingredients and to organize the cookware you will need. When you have assembled everything, you're ready to begin cooking.

Chicken in peanut sauce is served with cooked spinach on special occasions in Zimbabwe. (Recipe on page 64.)

The Careful Cook

Whenever you cook, there are certain safety rules you must always keep in mind. Even experienced cooks follow these rules when they are in the kitchen.

- Always wash your hands before handling food. Thoroughly wash all raw vegetables and fruits to remove dirt, chemicals, and insecticides. Wash uncooked poultry, meats, and fish under cold water before preparing.
- Use a cutting board when cutting up vegetables and fruits. Don't cut them up in your hand! And be sure to cut in a direction *away* from you and your fingers.
- Long hair or loose clothing can easily catch fire if brought near the burners of a stove. If you have long hair, tie it back before you start cooking.
- Turn all pot handles toward the back of the stove so that you will not catch your sleeves or jewelry on them. This is especially important when younger brothers and sisters are around. They could easily knock off a pot and get burned.
- Always use a pot holder to steady hot pots or to take pans out of the oven. Don't use a wet cloth on a hot pan because the steam it produces could burn you.
- Lift the lid of a steaming pot with the opening away from you so that you will not get burned.
- If you get burned, hold the burn under cold running water. Do not put grease or butter on it. Cold water helps to take the heat out, but grease or butter will only keep it in.
- If grease or cooking oil catches fire, throw baking soda or salt at the bottom of the flame to put it out. (Water will *not* put out a grease fire.) Call for help, and try to turn all the stove burners to "off."

Cooking Utensils

bamboo skewers—Long, thin wooden sticks used for roasting meat or vegetables over hot coals

colander—A bowl with holes in the bottom and sides. It is used for washing food or draining liquid from a solid food.

cooling rack—A wire rack upon which foods can be placed for cooling

Dutch oven—A heavy pot with a tightly fitting lid. Dutch ovens are often used for cooking soups or stews.

meat thermometer—A thermometer designed for testing the interior temperature of a cut of meat. To use, insert the thermometer into the center of the meat, but do not allow it to touch the pan.

rubber scraper—A flexible rubber utensil used to scrape food from the side of a bowl

Cooking Terms

beat—To stir rapidly in a circular motion

broil—To cook food under a direct flame

brown—To cook food quickly over high heat until surface browns

core— To remove the core (central part) from a fruit or vegetable

fold—To blend an ingredient with other ingredients by using a gentle overturning motion instead of by stirring or beating

grate—To shred food into tiny pieces by rubbing it against a grater

marinate—To soak food in a seasoned liquid to flavor and tenderize it

mince—To chop food into very small pieces

puree—To mash food to a smooth blend, paste, or thick liquid. The mashed substance is also referred to as a puree.

sauté—To fry quickly in oil or fat over high heat, stirring or turning the food to prevent burning

seed—To remove seeds from a food

sift—To mix several dry ingredients together or remove lumps in dry ingredients by putting them through a tool called a sifter

simmer—To cook over low heat in liquid kept just below its boiling point. Bubbles may occasionally rise to the surface.

thread—To slide a skewer through the center of a piece of meat, fruit, or vegetable, in preparation for grilling or broiling

zest—To scrape the peel from a lemon or other citrus fruit using a cheese grater or a special utensil called a zester

Special Ingredients

allspice—A mild spice made from the berries of the allspice tree

apple cider vinegar—Vinegar made from apple juice

bay leaf—The dried leaf of the bay (also called laurel) tree. It is used to season food.

black-eyed peas—Small, tan-colored peas with a large black spot (from which they get their name). Sometimes called cowpeas, these legumes are available canned, dried, or fresh.

cardamom—A spice from the ginger family, used whole or ground to give food a sweet, cool taste

cassava—A starchy root vegetable that can either be cooked or ground into flour

chutney—A thick, jellylike condiment made by cooking dried or fresh fruits and vegetables with vinegar and sugar

cloves—The highly fragrant dried flower buds of a tropical tree of the myrtle family, used whole or ground as a spice

coconut milk—The white, milky liquid extracted from coconut meat and used to flavor foods. Reduced-fat (light) coconut milk can be substituted for regular coconut milk in many recipes.

cream-style corn—Pureed sweet corn available in cans

cumin—The seeds of an herb used whole or ground to give food a pungent, slightly hot flavor

curry powder—A mixture made from spices such as turmeric, cumin, coriander, and others that is used to season foods

gingerroot—The knobby, light brown root of a tropical plant, used to flavor food. To use fresh ginger, slice off the amount called for, peel off the skin, and grate the flesh. Freeze the rest of the root for future use. Do not substitute dried ground ginger for fresh ginger, as the taste is very different.

natural peanut butter—A pure form of the American favorite, made with crushed peanuts, peanut oil, and sometimes salt, and available in the health food section or the refrigerated section of grocery stores

peanut oil—Oil made from pressed peanuts that is used to fry foods

raw peanuts—Peanuts that have not been roasted, salted, or flavored in any way

red pepper flakes—The dried seeds and skin of a hot red pepper, used to make foods spicy

samp—dried, white hominy corn

self-rising flour—Flour that already has baking powder and salt added to it

tamarind paste—A paste made from the fruit of the tamarind tree, native to Asia. Look for tamarind paste at Asian and African markets.

turmeric—A yellow spice made from the root of the turmeric plant

vanilla bean—Long black beans from the orchid plant, used to add a rich, sweet flavor to food. Vanilla beans should be removed from foods before serving.

vanilla extract—Concentrated liquid flavoring made from vanilla beans

white cornmeal—a coarse flour made from ground, dried white corn (instead of yellow) and used to make porridge or bread

zest—The outer, brightly colored peel of citrus fruits such as lemons

Healthy and Low-Fat Cooking Tips

Southern African cooking is rich with stews, cornmeal porridges, barbecued meat and seafood, and lots of fresh fruits and vegetables. These foods can form the basis of a healthy diet. Following are a few general tips for making most of these dishes even healthier. Throughout the book, you'll also find specific suggestions for individual recipes—and don't worry, they'll still taste delicious!

Many recipes call for butter or oil to sauté ingredients. Using oil lowers saturated fat, but you can also reduce the amount of oil you use. Sprinkling a little salt on vegetables brings out their juices, so less oil is needed. It's also a good idea to use a nonstick frying pan if you decide to use less oil than the recipe calls for. Or you can substitute a low-fat or nonfat cooking spray for oil. Another common substitution for butter is margarine. Before making this change, consider the recipe. If it is a dessert, it's often best to use butter. Margarine may noticeably change the food's taste or consistency.

Dairy products can be another source of unwanted fat. Try replacing heavy cream with half-and-half or whole milk in nonbaked dishes. Coconut milk, an ingredient used in southern African cooking, is high in fat, but you can often use reduced-fat or "light" varieties.

Some cooks replace red meat with chicken, turkey, or chunks of tofu to lower the fat content. However, since this does change the flavor, you may need to experiment a bit to decide if you like these substitutions. Buying extra-lean cuts of meat and trimming visible fat are also easy ways to reduce fat. When recipes call for chicken broth, you may want to use low-fat or vegetable broth instead. In dishes containing eggs, you can lower cholesterol content by using an egg substitute.

There are many ways to prepare healthy meals that still taste great. As you become a more experienced cook, try experimenting with recipes and substitutions to find the methods that work best for you.

METRIC CONVERSIONS

Cooks in the United States measure both liquid and solid ingredients using standard containers based on the 8-ounce cup and the tablespoon. These measurements are based on volume, while the metric system of measurement is based on both weight (for solids) and volume (for liquids). To convert from U.S. fluid tablespoons, ounces, quarts, and so forth to metric liters is a straightforward conversion, using the chart below. However, since solids have different weights—one cup of rice does not weigh the same as one cup of grated cheese, for example—many cooks who use the metric system have kitchen scales to weigh different ingredients. The chart below will give you a good starting point for basic conversions to the metric system.

MASS (weight)

1 ounce (oz.)	=	28.0 grams (g)
8 ounces	=	227.0 grams
1 pound (lb.) or 16 ounces	=	0.45 kilograms (kg)
2.2 pounds	=	1.0 kilogram

LIQUID VOLUME

1 teaspoon (tsp.)	=	5.0 milliliters (ml)
1 tablespoon (tbsp.)	=	15.0 milliliters
1 fluid ounce (oz.)	=	30.0 milliliters
1 cup (c.)	=	240 milliliters
1 pint (pt.)	=	480 milliliters
1 quart (qt.)	=	0.95 liters (l)
1 gallon (gal.)	=	3.80 liters

LENGTH

¼ inch (in.)	=	0.6 centimeters (cm)
½ inch	=	1.25 centimeters
1 inch	=	2.5 centimeters

TEMPERATURE

212°F	=	100°C (boiling point of water)
225°F	=	110°C
250°F	=	120°C
275°F	=	135°C
300°F	=	150°C
325°F	=	160°C
350°F	=	180°C
375°F	=	190°C
400°F	=	200°C

(To convert temperature in Fahrenheit to Celsius, subtract 32 and multiply by .56)

PAN SIZES

8-inch cake pan	=	20 x 4-centimeter cake pan
9-inch cake pan	=	23 x 3.5-centimeter cake pan
11 x 7-inch baking pan	=	28 x 18-centimeter baking pan
13 x 9-inch baking pan	=	32.5 x 23-centimeter baking pan
9 x 5-inch loaf pan	=	23 x 13-centimeter loaf pan
2-quart casserole	=	2-liter casserole

A Southern African Table

In small African villages, families traditionally meet for dinner in small outdoor courtyards that are used for eating and for cooking over a wood-stoked fire. Cooks set earthenware pots filled with foods such as cornmeal porridge, spinach in peanut sauce, meat and vegetable stews, and black-eyed peas on the ground, and diners gather around. Diners all eat from the same pots. Usually, they begin by dipping a hand into the porridge, taking a handful of the stiff cornmeal mixture, hollowing it out, and using it as a "spoon" to scoop up cooked vegetables or stewed meats.

In southern African cities or in the homes of southern Africans of European descent, dining experiences can be quite different. For example, dinnertime in Mozambique may be a more formal affair, heavily influenced by Portuguese traditions. The table, covered with a lace tablecloth, might be decorated with candles and fresh flowers. And on every dinner table in Mozambique, diners find a small bowl filled with piri-piri, a spicy, hot-pepper powder used to season food. Adults usually have a glass of wine with dinner. On special occasions, many Afrikaners and southern Africans of British descent dress the table in pressed white linens, setting it with fine china and silverware. A bowl of fruit may adorn the center of the table, along with condiments such as salt, pepper, vinegar, and steak sauce. But for everyday meals, they're likely to set a more casual table—often outside, where they can enjoy the warm, sunny weather.

A family in South Africa prepares a meal over a small cooking fire.

A Southern African Menu

A typical southern African menu is difficult to define, because of the tremendous amount of variety in the region. The following dinner menus combine dishes from all over southern Africa. The first menu includes a meat-based main dish, while the second is vegetarian.

DINNER #1

Sweet corn soup

Curried meatloaf

Cornmeal with pumpkin and peanut butter

Spinach with peanut sauce

Cassava sweet

SHOPPING LIST:

Produce

3 medium onions
3 lb. fresh spinach
1 red bell pepper
1 lemon
1 apple
1 lb. cassava

Dairy/Egg/Meat

1 qt. milk
¼ lb. (1 stick) butter
1 pt. heavy cream
2 eggs
1 lb. lean ground beef or lamb

Canned/Bottled/Boxed

16-oz. can chicken or vegetable stock
12-oz. can vegetable stock
16-oz. can cream-style sweet corn
16-oz. can pureed pumpkin
16-oz. can reduced-fat coconut milk
1 jar creamy, natural peanut butter
prepared chutney
apple cider vinegar
canola oil

Miscellaneous

1 slice crusty white bread
½ c. slivered almonds
½ c. chopped dried apricots
½ c. raisins
yellow cornmeal
mild curry powder
cinnamon
celery salt
bay leaves
red pepper flakes
sugar
salt
black pepper

DINNER #2

Avocado, peanut, and ginger salad

Vegetable stew

Stiff porridge

Black-eyed peas

Sweet potato cookies

SHOPPING LIST:

Produce

2 avocados
1 medium onion
1 large and one medium sweet potato
1 carrot
1 red bell pepper
½ c. green beans (fresh or frozen)
4 c. black-eyed peas (or canned)
1 small lemon
1 bulb garlic
1-inch piece gingerroot

Dairy/Egg/Meat

1 c. milk (unless using water)
2 sticks butter
1 egg

Canned/Bottled/Boxed

lemon juice (or 1 fresh lemon)
3 tsp. tomato paste
16-oz. can vegetable stock
honey
canola oil

Miscellaneous

½ c. raw, unsalted peanuts
white cornmeal
all-purpose flour
baking powder
baking soda
turmeric
paprika
cumin
red pepper flakes
nutmeg
sugar
salt

Staples

Corn, as the most common staple in southern Africa, is likely to make an appearance in some shape or form at nearly every meal. People throughout the region may start the day with a bowl of sugar-sweetened cornmeal porridge, enjoy a bowl of savory porridge and vegetables for lunch, snack on roasted corn on the cob in the afternoon, and eat samp and beans with grilled steak or chicken for dinner.

Wheat, rice, and other grains have also made their way into southern African cuisine. Afrikaners, for example, enjoy rusks—crunchy, dried wheat biscuits, sometimes spiked with raisins and nuts—dipped in coffee for breakfast. Many people also like eating fresh rusks when they are still soft and moist.

Stiff porridge (top) is a simple dish that can be dressed up as cornmeal with pumpkin and peanut butter (bottom) and served with fresh spinach. (Recipes on pages 34 and 35.)

Rusks/Beskuit (South Africa)

Many South Africans make rusks themselves, but when in a rush, they can also buy them already made, either dried out or still in moist loaf form. They are equally delicious either way.

2 c. unbleached white flour

2 c. whole wheat flour

⅓ c. brown sugar

½ tsp. salt

2 tsp. baking powder

1 tsp. cinnamon

½ c. unsalted sunflower seeds, shelled

½ c. raisins

½ c. (1 stick) butter, melted

2 eggs, beaten

¾ c. buttermilk

1. Preheat oven to 350°F.

2. In a large mixing bowl, mix together flours, sugar, salt, baking powder, cinnamon, sunflower seeds, and raisins.

3. In a separate bowl, combine butter, eggs, and buttermilk.

4. Add buttermilk mixture to flour mixture and stir until well blended. The dough should be soft and slightly moist.

5. Form dough into 1-inch balls. Place them side by side, allowing them to touch each other, in a greased loaf pan. Bake for 45 minutes, or until the tops are crisp and beginning to brown.*

6. Reduce heat to 200°F and bake for 1 hour longer. The rusks will be very dry and hard. Allow to cool completely and store in a sealed container for up to 3 weeks.

*If you'd prefer soft, breadlike rusks, remove them from the oven at this point. Break them apart while still warm and enjoy them with butter or jam.

Makes 24 rusks
Preparation time: 20 minutes
Baking time: 1 hour and 45 minutes

Stiff Porridge/*Oshifima* (Namibia)

Oshifima is a Namibian version of the cornmeal porridge served throughout southern Africa. In Botswana the dish is called putu, while in Lesotho it is called papa. Namibians typically take a handful of the thick porridge, hollow out the center, and use it to spoon up the main course.

1 c. water

1 c. milk or water

1¼ c. white cornmeal

1. Bring water to a boil in a small saucepan. Meanwhile, pour milk into a medium bowl. Slowly add ¾ c. of the cornmeal to the milk, stirring constantly until the mixture has a pastelike consistency.

2. Carefully pour cornmeal mixture from the bowl into the boiling water, stirring to combine. Continue to stir, cooking for 4 or 5 minutes. Add remaining ½ c. cornmeal, and stir until the porridge thickens and pulls away from the sides of the pan.

3. Use a rubber scraper to scrape porridge into a lightly greased serving bowl. When it's cool enough to handle, use your hands to shape the porridge into a ball and place it in the center of the bowl. Serve immediately.

Serves 4
Preparation time: 5 minutes
Cooking time: 15 to 20 minutes

Cornmeal with Pumpkin and Peanut Butter/ Nhopi (Zimbabwe)

In Zimbabwe, cooks add pumpkin and peanut butter to standard cornmeal porridge to create a healthy, substantial meal.

2 c. water

I c. yellow cornmeal

I 16-oz. can pureed pumpkin

I tsp. sugar

2 tbsp. creamy, natural peanut
   butter

½ tsp. salt

I lb. fresh spinach, washed, stems
   removed

1. In a medium saucepan, boil the water. Add cornmeal, stir, and reduce heat to a simmer.

2. Cook for about 10 minutes, stirring often, until mixture thickens. Add pumpkin, sugar, peanut butter, and salt, and mix thoroughly. Remove from heat and serve with fresh spinach on the side.

Serves 4
Preparation time: 5 minutes
Cooking time: 20 to 25 minutes

Soups, Salads, and Side Dishes

The abundance of fruits and vegetables that thrive in southern Africa's warm climate forms the basis of stews and provides nice accompaniments to the grilled meat dishes that are so popular in the region. Pumpkin, yams, and spinach native to the African continent mix with the corn, tomatoes, and peppers that were introduced later during trade with South America to create excellent side dishes, soups, and salads. In addition, southern Africans of Asian descent have contributed rice to the area's cuisine, and it may be served plain or flavored with curry spices and dried fruits.

Peanuts, known as groundnuts in their native Africa, play a prominent role in side dishes, adding flavor and protein. Cooks use peanuts in a variety of ways. They may crush them to sprinkle as a garnish over salads such as the avocado, peanut, and ginger salad, or mash the nuts and mix them with vegetable stock to create delicious sauces. For a satisfying vegetarian meal, consider filling a buffet table with three or four of these dishes along with a cornmeal porridge.

Avocado, peanut, and ginger salad is a fresh, summery dish from Swaziland. (Recipe on page 39.)

Sweet Corn Soup (Botswana)

This creamy soup is a popular dish among workers and guests on southern Botswana's game farms, where herds of fabulous animals, from antelopes to giraffes, roam across the landscape.

2 c. milk

2 tbsp. butter

½ medium onion, chopped

1 tbsp. cornmeal

2 c. chicken or vegetable stock*

1 16-oz. can cream-style sweet corn

½ tsp. celery salt

½ tsp. black pepper

⅓ c. heavy cream**

1. In a medium saucepan, heat milk on low heat, taking care not to let it boil.

2. As the milk heats, warm butter in a kettle over medium heat. Add onion and sauté for 5 minutes, stirring frequently, until onion is translucent and soft.

3. Reduce heat to low and add cornmeal to kettle. Cook for about 2 minutes, stirring constantly.

4. Turn off heat and slowly stir warm milk into onion mixture.

5. Turn heat back on to medium and add chicken or vegetable stock, corn, celery salt, and pepper. Bring soup to a boil, stirring often. Reduce heat to low and add cream. Stir to combine and cook until heated through, about 5 more minutes.

*To lower this soup's fat content, use reduced-fat broth.

**Half-and-half and whole milk are both suitable substitutes for cream if you'd like to cut fat from this recipe, although it will not be as rich and creamy.

Serves 4 to 6
Preparation time: 5 minutes
Cooking time: 20 minutes

Avocado, Peanut, and Ginger Salad (Swaziland)

Cool and refreshing, this salad of creamy avocado cubes, crunchy peanuts, and spicy ginger is a favorite in Swaziland.

2 tbsp. lemon juice

1 tsp. freshly grated gingerroot*

½ tsp. salt

2 avocados, pitted, peeled, and cubed**

½ c. finely chopped raw, unsalted peanuts

1. In a medium serving bowl, mix lemon juice, gingerroot, and salt.

2. Add avocado and stir gently to coat thoroughly with the lemon juice mixture. Set aside for at least 30 minutes.

3. Just before serving, sprinkle salad with peanuts.

Serves 4
Preparation time: 10 minutes
Marinating time: 30 minutes

To peel ginger, use a vegetable peeler or the edge of a spoon to remove the root's thin skin. Grate the flesh with a ginger grater or fine cheese grater. Skinned ginger can also be chopped up finely with a knife.

**To pit, peel, and cube an avocado, slice it in half lengthwise, carefully working around the pit. Split the two sides apart by twisting them slightly in opposite directions. Remove the pit and use a knife to lightly cut the flesh into ½-inch cubes. Press upward from the skin side through the middle of each half, turning the fruit inside out. Use a knife to gently separate the avocado cubes from the skin.*

Samp and Beans/Umngqusho (Botswana, South Africa)

4 c. dry samp (white hominy corn)*

2 c. dried black-eyed peas**

1 tbsp. canola oil

1 large onion, sliced

2 cloves garlic, minced

½ tsp. ground cloves

½ tsp. allspice

¼ tsp. nutmeg

½ tsp. salt

½ tsp. black pepper

3 tbsp. butter (optional)

*Look for samp at African or Mexican markets, or even your local supermarket.

**In this recipe, the "beans" are actually black-eyed peas, but cooks prepare many variations of the dish. You can also use canned peas in this recipe. Rinse them well, and don't add them to the pot until Step 2, after the samp has been cooking for about 45 minutes.

1. Combine samp and black-eyed peas in a large bowl. Add enough cold water to cover. Refrigerate (covered) overnight. Once while peas are soaking, rub them gently between your palms to remove skins. When skins float to the top, remove with a slotted spoon and discard. Drain and rinse well before cooking.

2. In a large pot, cover samp and black-eyed peas with cold water and bring to a boil. Boil 10 minutes, reduce heat to low, and simmer 1 to 2 hours, or until peas and samp are tender and water is mostly absorbed. Add more water during cooking if needed.

3. While samp and peas simmer, heat oil in a medium-sized skillet. Sauté onion and garlic for 5 minutes, or until soft. Add cloves and allspice, stir, and cook for another minute.

4. Add onion mixture to samp and beans. Stir to combine. Continue cooking until soft. Season with nutmeg, salt, and black pepper. Stir in butter, if desired, and serve hot.

Serves 6 to 8
Preparation time: 10 minutes
(plus overnight soaking time)
Cooking time: about 2 hours

Black-eyed Peas (Namibia)

In Africa, this dish is traditionally made with cowpeas, a slightly smaller but very similar legume that grows well on the African continent. If you cannot find fresh black-eyed peas, substitute canned peas.

4 c. fresh black-eyed peas*

1 tsp. salt

½ tsp. red pepper flakes

1. In a kettle or large bowl, soak fresh peas in cold water for 5 minutes, or until they soften. Allowing peas to continue soaking, rub them gently between your palms to help remove the skins. When the skins float to the top, use a slotted spoon to remove them.

2. Pour water and skinless peas into a colander to drain. Rinse peas with cold water.

3. Place peas in a Dutch oven and add enough fresh water to cover them. Add salt and red pepper flakes and bring to a boil over high heat.

4. Turn heat down to a simmer and cook peas for about 1 hour, or until they can be easily pierced with a fork. To serve, spoon peas and a little bit of the cooking water over stiff porridge or cornmeal with pureed pumpkin and peanut butter. (See pages 34 and 35 for recipes.)

*To save time, substitute canned black-eyed peas for fresh. Rinse well and place in a pot or Dutch oven. Add salt, red pepper flakes, and 3½ cups water. Place over medium heat and simmer 10 to 15 minutes, or until warmed through. Serve as suggested in Step 4.

Serves 6 to 8
Preparation time: 20 minutes
Cooking time: 1 hour

Yellow Rice with Raisins/Geelrys met Rosyne (South Africa)

The turmeric, raisins, and lemon zest in this recipe transform ordinary rice into a special treat that's easy to make. This rice is traditionally served with curried meatloaf, and it also goes well with grilled lamb, pork, and apricot skewers.

3 c. water

2 tbsp. sugar

1 tsp. turmeric

1 tsp. salt

1 tbsp. butter

1 stick cinnamon

½ c. raisins

1 tsp. lemon zest*

1 c. short-grain white rice

1. In a medium saucepan, combine water, sugar, turmeric, salt, butter, cinnamon, raisins, and lemon zest. Mix and bring to a boil over high heat.

2. Add rice and stir to combine. Cover, reduce heat to a simmer, and cook for about 25 minutes, or until water is absorbed and the rice is tender. Serve hot.

Serves 4
Preparation time: 5 minutes
Cooking time 30 minutes

*Wash the lemon well before zesting.
If you do not have a zesting tool, use a
fine cheese grater to remove only the thin,
yellow layer of the peel, avoiding as much
of the bitter white pith as possible.

Main Dishes

Throughout southern Africa, most people cannot afford to eat meat every day. As a result, vegetable stews made from chopped onions, carrots, sweet potatoes, tomatoes, bell peppers, and spinach are very popular and are usually served with a thick, seasoned cornmeal porridge. Peanuts are featured in many entres, too, often as part of a flavorful sauce served over spinach, other vegetables, or meat. When meat is available, tossing bite-sized pieces into a stew allows cooks to divide a small amount among many people. In Mozambique, where seafood is plentiful, the clam and peanut stew called matata is a favorite. In Zimbabwe, steak and bean stew, known as nyama ne nyemba, and chicken and peanut stew, called dovi, are specialties that are often reserved for celebratory feasts.

Where available, grilled meats take center stage. Beef and lamb steaks are popular in Botswana, Zimbabwe, and South Africa, while grilled shrimp in a spicy piri-piri sauce is common in Mozambique. South Africans are very fond of grilled boerewors and of sosaties— marinated meat kebabs that are served with fruit chutneys.

South Africans combine lamb, pork, and dried apricots on skewers to create this sweet and savory dish, perfect for grilling. (Recipe on page 46.)

Lamb, Pork, and Apricot Skewers/ *Sosaties* (South Africa)

This unique dish is a barbecue favorite among South Africans. Curry seasoning, combined with dried fruit, reflects the strong influence of the Cape Malay people on regional cuisine.

1 clove garlic, peeled and crushed, and 2 cloves minced

1 lb. lamb, cut into 1-inch cubes

1 lb. pork, cut into 1-inch cubes

½ tsp. salt

½ tsp. black pepper

2 tbsp. olive oil

1 medium onion, chopped

1 tbsp. curry powder

2 tbsp. sugar

1 tbsp. tamarind paste

2 c. apple cider vinegar

2 tbsp. apricot jam

½ lb. dried apricots

½ c. boiling water

1. Rub the inside of a large glass bowl with crushed garlic and discard garlic. Place lamb and pork pieces in the bowl, add salt and pepper, and stir to combine seasonings. Set aside.

2. Heat oil in a medium-sized saucepan over medium heat. Add onion and sauté for about 5 minutes, or until soft and translucent.

3. Add curry powder and minced garlic and cook for 1 minute, stirring to coat onion evenly with curry powder.

4. Stir in sugar, tamarind paste, vinegar, and jam. Cook, stirring constantly, until mixture thickens (10 to 15 minutes). Remove pan from heat.

5. When mixture has cooled completely (about 20 to 30 minutes), pour it over the meat. Cover bowl with plastic wrap and place in the refrigerator to marinate for 1 to 2 days.

6. About one hour before you plan to cook the meat, ask an adult to help you prepare the grill.* Drain marinade from meat into a small saucepan. Then combine dried apricots with boiling water in a small bowl. Let sit 30 minutes and drain.

7. Thread alternating pieces of lamb, pork, and apricots onto bamboo skewers. Grill for about 15 minutes, turning the meat to allow it to brown on all sides.

8. While grilling, heat reserved marinade over medium heat. Remove meat and fruit from skewers, and serve together with marinade over rice.

*This dish can also be cooked on a cookie sheet under the broiler of an oven.

Serves 4 to 6
Preparation time: 1 to 1½ hours
(Plus 1 to 2 days marinating time)
Grilling time: 15 minutes

Clam and Peanut Stew/Matata (Mozambique)

This dish combines the abundant seafood for which Mozambique is known with peanuts, which are so popular throughout Africa.

2 tbsp. olive oil

1 medium onion, chopped finely

1 16-oz. can chopped clams, with juice

½ c. chopped raw, unsalted peanuts

2 medium tomatoes, peeled, seeded, and chopped (about 1 c.)*

1 tsp. salt

½ tsp. black pepper

1 tsp. red pepper flakes

1 lb. fresh baby spinach, thoroughly washed, patted dry, and chopped finely

1. In a Dutch oven or kettle, warm oil over medium heat. Add onions and sauté, stirring often, for 5 to 7 minutes, or until onions are soft and translucent.

2. Add clams, peanuts, tomatoes, salt, black pepper, and red pepper. Stir to combine. Cover and simmer for 30 minutes.

3. Add spinach and stir. Cover pot again and cook 2 to 3 minutes longer, or until spinach has wilted. Serve hot with white rice.

Serves 4
Preparation time: 15 minutes
Cooking time: 40 to 45 minutes

*To peel a tomato, use a knife to score (very lightly cut)
a small "x" in the top. Place the tomato in a small
saucepan of boiling water for about 1 minute. Remove
with a slotted spoon and cool until the tomato is warm but
no longer hot. Use a small paring knife to peel off the
skin. It will come off easily. As you chop the tomatoes, use
the knife to remove as many of the seeds as possible.

Curried Meatloaf/Bobotie (South Africa)

1¼ c. milk

1 slice crusty white bread

½ c. slivered almonds

1 tbsp. butter

1 medium onion, chopped

2 eggs

1 lb. lean ground beef or lamb

2 tsp. mild curry powder

3 tbsp. fresh lemon juice

½ c. chopped dried apricots

½ c. raisins

½ apple, cored, peeled, and chopped

2 tbsp. prepared fruit chutney

½ tsp. salt

½ tsp. black pepper

2 bay leaves

*Bobotie is done when a meat thermometer inserted into the center of the loaf reads 160°F for beef or 180°F for lamb.

1. Preheat oven to 350°F. In a medium bowl, pour milk over bread. Let soak for 30 minutes.

2. Spread almonds evenly across a cookie sheet. Bake 5 to 7 minutes, or until golden brown. Remove from oven and allow to cool.

3. Melt butter in a medium-sized skillet over medium heat. Add onion and sauté 5 minutes, or until soft. Remove from heat.

4. Squeeze the milk from the bread. Leaving milk in the bowl, set bread aside. Add eggs to milk and beat with a whisk or fork. Set aside.

5. In a large bowl, use your hands to combine bread, meat, curry powder, lemon juice, almonds, apricots, raisins, apple, chutney, salt, and pepper. Add onion and half of the egg mixture to meat mixture and combine thoroughly.

6. Use a rubber scraper to scrape meat mixture from bowl into a greased 9 × 5-inch loaf pan. Press bay leaves onto top of loaf and pour remaining egg mixture over all. Bake for about 1½ to 2 hours, or until done.*

Serves 4
Preparation time: 45 minutes
(plus 30 minutes soaking time)
Baking time: 1½ to 2 hours

Vegetable Stew (Botswana)

This delicious dish is easy to make and quite nutritious. If you don't have all of the vegetables called for in the recipe, feel free to substitute others, such as red potatoes, butternut squash, peas, or celery.

1 tbsp. canola oil

1 medium onion, chopped

½ tsp. turmeric

½ tsp. paprika

1 tsp. cumin

2 cloves garlic, minced

1 tbsp. freshly peeled and grated gingerroot*

3 tsp. tomato paste

1 large sweet potato, peeled and chopped

1 carrot, peeled and chopped

½ red bell pepper, cored, seeded, and chopped

½ c. fresh or frozen green beans, ends trimmed

2 c. vegetable stock

1. In a Dutch oven or large kettle, warm oil over medium heat. Add onion and sauté for about 5 minutes, or until soft and translucent.

2. Add turmeric, paprika, cumin, garlic, gingerroot, and tomato paste. Mix well and cook for 1 minute.

3. Add sweet potato, carrot, red bell pepper, and green beans. Stir well to coat vegetables with spices.

4. Add stock and bring to a boil over high heat. Reduce heat and simmer, partially covered, for about 30 minutes, or until tender. Serve hot over stiff porridge (see recipe on page 34).

Serves 4
Preparation time: 15 to 20 minutes
Cooking time: 45 minutes

*To peel ginger, use a vegetable peeler or the edge of a spoon to remove the root's thin skin. Grate the flesh with a ginger grater or fine cheese grater. Skinned ginger can also be chopped up finely with a knife.

Spinach with Peanut Sauce (Zimbabwe)

This dish makes a great vegetarian entrée. It can also be served as a tasty accompaniment to a heartier meat-based main course.

½ c. creamy, natural peanut butter

2 tbsp. apple cider vinegar

½ tsp. salt

½ tsp. red pepper flakes

2 tbsp. canola oil

1 large onion, sliced thinly

1 red bell pepper, cored, seeded, and chopped

1½ c. vegetable stock

2 lb. fresh spinach, washed, stems removed, and coarsely chopped

1. In a medium bowl, combine peanut butter, vinegar, salt, and red pepper.

2. In a large Dutch oven or kettle, heat oil over medium heat. Sauté onion and red bell pepper for about 5 minutes, stirring often.

3. Add vegetable stock, raise heat to high, and bring to a boil. Stir in peanut butter mixture.

4. Add spinach and cook, stirring often, for about 5 minutes, or until spinach begins to become limp. Serve hot with stiff porridge (see recipe on page 34).

Serves 4
Preparation time: 10 minutes
Cooking time: 20 to 25 minutes

Desserts

Desserts weren't common in southern Africa before the arrival of European settlers. If native southern Africans craved something sweet, they usually reached for fresh fruits such as watermelon, mangoes, papayas, or coconuts. However, German, Dutch, French, British, and Scandinavian newcomers brought a taste for rich desserts and contributed the cakes, puddings, and tarts that provide sweet endings to many modern southern African meals.

Nevertheless, most of the recipes included in this book are uniquely African, using native fruits and vegetables such as cassava, coconut, pumpkin, and sweet potato to create European-style desserts. A recipe for fruit salad, glazed with a sweet vanilla syrup, stays in the traditional spirit of ending the meal with a simple piece of fruit.

These British-influenced sweet potato cookies are a teatime favorite in Zimbabwe. (Recipe on page 57.)

Cassava Sweet/Doce de Mandioca (Mozambique)

Cassava, a starchy root that grows easily in the dry, desertlike conditions in southern Africa, is the basis of many meals in traditional African households. This recipe transforms the ordinary vegetable into a sweet dessert.

1 lb. sweet cassava, peeled and cut into ½-inch pieces*

1 16-oz. can reduced-fat coconut milk

1½ c. sugar

2 tsp. cinnamon

1. Place cassava and coconut milk in a medium saucepan over low heat. While stirring, slowly add sugar. Cook, stirring often, for 30 minutes, or until cassava is very tender and mixture has thickened.

2. Once mixture is thick, cook for 3 minutes more and remove from heat. Allow to cool completely.

3. Transfer cassava mixture to a glass serving bowl. Sprinkle the top with cinnamon and serve at room temperature.

Serves 6
Preparation time: 10 minutes
Cooking time: 25 to 30 minutes
Cooling time: 30 minutes

*Peeling cassava is similar to peeling a potato but can be more difficult since the root is tougher. Ask an adult if you need any help. You can also look for frozen sweet cassava at your grocery store or at African markets.

Sweet Potato Cookies (Zimbabwe)

British cooks in southern Africa combined their love of teatime sweets with the African sweet potato to create these delicious cookies.

10 tbsp. butter (1¼ sticks), softened

¼ c. sugar

1 tbsp. lemon zest*

1 tsp. nutmeg

¼ c. honey

1 egg

1 medium sweet potato, peeled and grated

2½ c. flour

1½ tsp. baking powder

½ tsp. baking soda

½ tsp. salt

1. Preheat oven to 350°F.

2. In a large mixing bowl, use an electric mixer to combine butter and sugar. Add lemon zest, nutmeg, honey, and egg, stirring thoroughly to combine. Using a rubber scraper, fold sweet potato into the butter and sugar mixture.

3. Sift flour, baking powder, baking soda, and salt into a separate bowl. Gradually add the flour mixture to the sweet potato mixture, stirring well to combine thoroughly.

4. Place a rounded tablespoon of the dough onto an ungreased cookie sheet, spacing them about 1 inch apart. Bake for 7 to 10 minutes, or until lightly browned.

5. Use a spatula to transfer freshly baked cookies to a cooling rack. Store cooled cookies in an airtight container for up to one week.

*Wash the lemon well before zesting. If you do not have a zesting tool, use a fine cheese grater to remove only the thin, yellow layer of the peel, avoiding as much of the bitter white pith as possible.

Makes about 40 cookies
Preparation time: 10 to 15 minutes
Baking time: 7 to 10 minutes

Pumpkin Fritters/Pampoenkoekies (South Africa)

Fritters of all kinds are popular throughout Africa. African cooks mash up any abundant fruit or vegetable, mix it with flour and egg, and fry the batter in hot oil like doughnuts. Savory fritters are common, but cinnamon sugar turns this pumpkin version into a great dessert.

1 c. canned pumpkin

½ c. flour

1 egg, slightly beaten

½ tsp. salt

2 tbsp. sugar

½ tsp. cinnamon

peanut oil for frying*

1. In a large bowl, combine pumpkin, flour, egg, salt, and 1 tbsp. sugar. Mix well. The batter should resemble a thick paste and should keep its shape when scooped up in a tablespoon. If mixture is too thick and dry, add ¼ c. warm water. If it is too thin and runny, add ¼ c. flour.

2. In a small bowl, mix remaining sugar with cinnamon and set aside.

3. In a heavy saucepan or electric frying pan, heat 2 inches of oil to 375°F, or until a drop of water flicked into the pan jumps back out.

4. Carefully use a large serving spoon to drop a few spoonfuls of batter into the hot oil at a time. Cook for about 2 minutes on each side, or until lightly browned. Use a slotted spoon to remove fritters from hot oil and drain on paper towels. Lightly dust hot fritters with cinnamon-sugar mixture and serve immediately.

*Cooking with hot oil is simple and safe as long as you're careful and an adult is present. Be sure to use long-handled utensils whenever possible. Stand as far back from the stove as is comfortable, and lower batter into the oil as slowly as possible in order to prevent splattering.

Serves 6
Preparation time: 15 minutes
Cooking time: 25 minutes

African Fruit Salad

Fruits such as watermelon, pineapple, mangoes, and bananas are available throughout Africa and often serve as snacks. In this dish, they provide a sweet finish to a satisfying meal.

3 c. water

1½ c. sugar

1 vanilla bean, sliced in half

1 fresh mango

1 pt. strawberries

3 bananas

2 tsp. lemon juice

1 20-oz. can pineapple chunks in juice, drained

2 c. watermelon, seeded and cut into 1-inch pieces

1. In a medium saucepan, combine water, sugar, and vanilla bean over medium-high heat. Bring mixture to a boil and cook for 7 to 10 minutes, or until it thickens and becomes syrupy. Remove from heat and set aside to cool.

2. Chop mango* into bite-sized pieces. Remove strawberry stems, core, and cut the strawberries in half. Peel and slice bananas and sprinkle with lemon juice. Add all fruit to bowl and mix well.

3. Remove vanilla bean from syrup and discard. Pour syrup over fruit and stir well to coat thoroughly. Serve in individual bowls.

Serves 6 to 8
Preparation time: 15 minutes
Cooking time: 10 minutes

*To peel and cut a mango, set the fruit on a cutting board so the ridge (which covers the fruit's flat pit) is face up. Carefully use a sharp knife to make two cuts on either side of this ridge and parallel to it, slicing all the way through the fruit. Discard the pit and place the two halves on the cutting board, flesh-side up. Use the knife to score (lightly cut) the flesh of each half, creating a checkerboard pattern. Then, taking a half in your hand, press upward from center of the skin side to loosen the scored cubes of mango. Carefully use the knife to separate the fruit from the skin.

Holiday and Festival Food

In southern Africa, most people celebrate holidays by serving everyone's favorite foods, many of which are also served throughout the year. However, one common thread in most holiday celebrations or festivals is cooking and enjoying meals outdoors. South Africans typically fire up the braai and grill meats such as boerewors, steaks, shrimp, and lamb. Alongside the main dish, cooks may serve baked sweet potatoes and a traditional tomato and onion salad known as train smash. Cakes, cookies, and tarts typically end the meal. A milk tart, or *melktert*, inspired by Dutch and French desserts, is traditionally served for occasions that focus on children, such as christenings, naming ceremonies, and first Holy Communion celebrations.

In other southern African countries, including Zimbabwe, Botswana, and Mozambique, meat is often too expensive for most people—which makes it an even greater treat on special occasions. Simple, one-course meals are supplemented with a number of side dishes and sometimes dessert during events such as harvest festivals and independence day celebrations.

Milk tart is a rich South African sweet served at many festivals and celebrations. (Recipe on page 68.)

Chicken in Peanut Sauce/Dovi (Zimbabwe)

Zimbabweans who cannot afford meat on an everyday basis save recipes like this one, a favorite that features a spicy peanut sauce, for special occasions.

1 tbsp. canola oil

2 medium onions, chopped finely

2 cloves garlic, minced

1 tsp. salt

½ tsp. black pepper

½ tsp. red pepper flakes

1 large green bell pepper, cored, seeded, and chopped

2 skinless, boneless chicken breasts, cut into bite-sized pieces*

1 large fresh tomato, seeded and chopped, or 1 16-oz. can chopped tomatoes

2 c. water

6 tbsp. creamy, natural peanut butter

½ lb. fresh spinach, thoroughly washed and patted dry

*After handling raw chicken or other poultry, always remember to thoroughly wash your hands, utensils, and preparation area with soapy, hot water. Also, when checking chicken for doneness, it's a good idea to cut it open gently to make sure that the meat is white (not pink) all the way through.

1. In a Dutch oven or kettle, warm oil over medium heat. Add onions and sauté 5 minutes, or until translucent.

2. Add garlic, salt, black pepper, and red pepper flakes. Cook for about 3 minutes, stirring often. Add green pepper and chicken and stir. Cook 7 to 10 minutes, stirring often, to brown chicken on all sides. Add tomato and water. Reduce heat, cover, and simmer 5 to 10 minutes.

3. In a medium bowl, combine peanut butter with 2 tbsp. of liquid from cooking pot. Add half of this mixture to the pot. Simmer 30 minutes, or until chicken is cooked through.

4. Near the end of the 30 minutes, fill a medium saucepan with water and bring to a boil. Add spinach and cook 1 minute, or until tender. Drain spinach in a colander, transfer to a bowl, and combine with remaining peanut mixture. Remove chicken to a second serving dish, and serve greens alongside chicken.

Serves 4 to 6
Preparation time: 15 minutes
Cooking time: 1 hour

Steak and Bean Stew/Nyama Ne Nyemba (Zimbabwe)

This dish is a Zimbabwean classic. Serve it with cornmeal with pumpkin and peanut butter or with yellow rice for a very satisfying meal.

1 tbsp. canola oil

2 medium onions, sliced thinly

2 lb. shoulder steak, cut into 1-inch cubes

2 cloves garlic, minced

1 small chili pepper, seeded and minced*

3 tbsp. curry powder

2 medium tomatoes, peeled and diced

½ tsp. salt

½ tsp. black pepper

2 16-oz. cans cooked kidney beans with liquid

3 tbsp. freshly squeezed lemon juice

1. In a Dutch oven or kettle, warm oil over medium heat. Add onions and sauté for 5 to 7 minutes, or until soft and translucent.

2. Add steak and cook for about 5 minutes, stirring often. Reduce heat to medium low and cook for another 15 to 20 minutes, still stirring occasionally.

3. Add garlic, chili pepper, and curry powder. Stir to combine and cook for about 3 more minutes.

4. Add tomatoes and cook for another 3 minutes.

5. Add salt, black pepper, beans, and liquid from beans. Simmer over low heat for about 15 minutes.

6. Serve hot, drizzled with fresh lemon juice.

Serves 4 to 6
Preparation time: 15 minutes
Cooking time: 45 minutes to 1 hour

*If you are not used to eating spicy foods, you may want to choose a fairly mild pepper variety such as poblano or Anaheim. For a hotter dish, try peppers such as jalapeño or serrano. Be careful when working with hot peppers or chilies. The oil on the skin of the peppers can burn you, so wear rubber gloves while cutting the pepper, and be sure to remove all the seeds. Wash your hands well when you are done.

Vegetable Biryani (South Africa)

This flavorful dish is popular among South Africans of Indian descent and is one of the many foods likely to be served during Diwali, a Hindu festival.

2 tbsp. canola oil

2 large onions, sliced

1 2-inch piece fresh gingerroot, peeled and minced

10 cloves garlic, minced

1 tsp. cayenne pepper

½ c. dried lentils

1 c. frozen green peas, thawed

2 carrots, chopped

1 c. fresh or frozen green beans

5 c. water

3 medium tomatoes, chopped

6 whole cloves

1 4-inch cinnamon stick

6 cardamom pods, crushed

1 tsp. turmeric

3 sprigs fresh mint, leaves minced and stems discarded, or ½ tsp. dried mint

2 c. long-grain white rice

4 medium potatoes, peeled and chopped

1 tsp. salt

1. In a Dutch oven or kettle, warm oil over medium heat. Sauté onions 5 minutes, or until translucent. Use a slotted spoon to remove about one-third of the onions to a small bowl. Set aside.

2. Add ginger, garlic, and cayenne pepper. Cook 5 minutes, stirring constantly, and add lentils, peas, carrots, and green beans. Reduce heat to medium low and cook 15 minutes. If mixture begins to dry out or stick to pan, add ¼ c. water. Meanwhile, place water in a small saucepan or teapot. Heat to a boil.

3. Add tomatoes, cloves, cinnamon, cardamom, turmeric, and mint to Dutch oven and stir. Cook 5 minutes. Carefully add 1 c. of boiling water. Cover and simmer 10 minutes.

4. Add rice, potatoes, salt, and remaining hot water to Dutch oven. Cover and cook 20 minutes, or until rice is tender. Serve hot, garnished with remaining onions.

Serves 6
Preparation time: 20 to 25 minutes
Cooking time: about 1 hour

Milk Tart/Melktert (South Africa)

Melktert is traditionally served at the Malay Feast of the Orange Leaves. This celebration is held after the naming ceremony of a new baby, which in Cape Malay culture takes place seven days after a baby's birth. The tart is also an old favorite in the Afrikaans community, often served with tea after Nagmaal (Holy Communion) gatherings.

Pastry:

¼ c. (½ stick) butter, softened

2 tbsp. sugar

1 egg, separated*

1 c. self-rising flour

½ tsp. salt

1 tbsp. milk

Filling:

2 eggs, separated

¼ tsp. cream of tartar

2¼ c. milk

¼ c. sugar

¾ c. cake flour

½ tsp. salt

2 tbsp. butter

1 tsp. vanilla extract

½ tsp. cinnamon

1. Preheat oven to 350°F.

2. In a large mixing bowl, use an electric mixer to combine butter and sugar. Add egg yolk (discarding the white) and beat until light and fluffy. In a separate bowl, sift together flour and salt. Combine flour mixture with butter and sugar mixture, add milk, and stir until thoroughly combined.

3. Lightly oil a 9-inch cake pan and dust with flour. Use a spatula to press dough into the pan evenly. Set aside.

4. To make filling, combine egg whites and cream of tartar. Use an electric mixer to beat the mixture for about 10 minutes, or until soft peaks begin to form. Set aside.

5. Combine milk and sugar in a saucepan over medium heat. As milk warms, place cake flour in a small bowl. Use a ladle to scoop about 1 c. of warm milk from the pan and add to flour. Stir to combine. Transfer milk and flour mixture to saucepan and cook, stirring constantly.

6. Add egg yolks and salt to saucepan and stir to combine. Raise heat to medium high and bring milk mixture to a boil. Stirring frequently, cook 10 minutes, or until thickened. Remove from heat, add butter and vanilla, and set aside for 5 minutes to cool slightly. Gently fold in the lightly beaten egg whites.

7. Pour milk filling over the prepared pastry crust. Sprinkle with cinnamon and bake for 30 minutes, or until filling is firm.

Serves 8
Preparation time: 30 to 40 minutes
Baking time: 30 minutes

*To separate an egg, crack it cleanly on the edge of a nonplastic bowl. Holding the two halves of the eggshell over the bowl, gently pour the egg yolk back and forth between the two halves, letting the egg white drip into the bowl and being careful not to break the yolk. When most of the egg white has been separated, place the yolk in another bowl.

Index

About the Authors

Kari Cornell is an avid cook who loves to experiment with new recipes and cuisines. As an editor and coauthor of children's books for several years, Cornell is pleased to combine the two activities she enjoys most to write cookbooks for this series. In addition to *Cooking the Southern African Way*, Cornell is the author of *Cooking the Indonesian Way* and *Cooking the Turkish Way*.

Peter Thomas has diverse interests, such as traveling, collecting traditional South African recipes, web design, and photography. All of these complement each other as can be seen when visiting his award-winning website http://funkymunky.co.za. Thomas lives in South Africa. He retired from a career in banking and uses his free time to pursue his hobbies.

Photo Acknowledgments

The photographs in this book are used with permission of: © Peter Johnson/ CORBIS, pp. 2–3, © Romane P./CORBIS SYGMA, p. 9; © Walter and Louiseann Pietrowicz/September 8th Stock, pp. 4 (both), 5 (both), 6, 18, 30, 33, 36, 41, 44, 49, 50, 54, 58, 61, 62, and 67; © Stapleton Collection/CORBIS, p. 11; © Adrian Arbib/CORBIS, p. 12; © Rob Ponte; Gallo Images/CORBIS, p. 15; © David Turnley/CORBIS, p. 26.

Cover photos (front, back, and spine): © Walter and Louiseann Pietrowicz/ September 8th Stock.

The illustrations on pages 7, 19, 27, 31, 32, 37, 38, 39, 40, 42, 43, 45, 47, 48, 51, 52, 55, 56, 57, 59, 60, 63, 64, 65, and 69 are by Tim Seeley. The map on page 8 is by Bill Hauser.